For Emma
and Joe, Naomi, Eddie, Laura, Isaac, Elsie, and Emile.
And for all the doctors, nurses, physiotherapists,
occupational therapists, and hospital workers who saved my life
and have helped me get better.

MR

Text copyright © 2021 by Michael Rosen
Illustrations copyright © 2021 by Tony Ross

First US edition 2022
First published by Walker Books Ltd. (UK) 2021

Library of Congress Catalog Card Number 2021953480
ISBN 978-1-5362-2532-7

22 23 24 25 26 27 APS 10 9 8 7 6 5 4 3 2 1

Printed in Humen, Dongguan, China

This book was typeset in Bookman.
The illustrations were done in ink and watercolor.

Candlewick Press
99 Dover Street
Somerville, Massachusetts 02144

www.candlewick.com

Michael Rosen's STICKY McSTICKSTICK

The Friend Who Helped Me Walk Again

Michael Rosen

illustrated by

Tony Ross

CANDLEWICK PRESS

I was sick.
I was so sick I couldn't get up.

One day, three people came to my bedside
and said, "Today we're going to get you up."

They lifted me up,
one on one side,
one on the other,
one behind.

I gasped.
I panted.
My legs were shaking.

I pleaded with them to let me get back into bed.
"Please let me go back to bed!"

They let me.

The next day,
they came to my bedside again
and said, "We're going to get you up."

I gasped and panted.

They put a walker in front of me
and asked me to hold it.

I did.

I was still gasping and panting.
I held on to the walker.

They said, "See if you can move the walker forward."

I did.

Just a tiny bit.

But I gasped and panted some more.
And they put me back to bed.

The next day, they said that I should see if I could get
from the walker to a wheelchair.

All three of them helped me.

We did it.

I liked the wheelchair.
I wheeled around the room
and the halls.

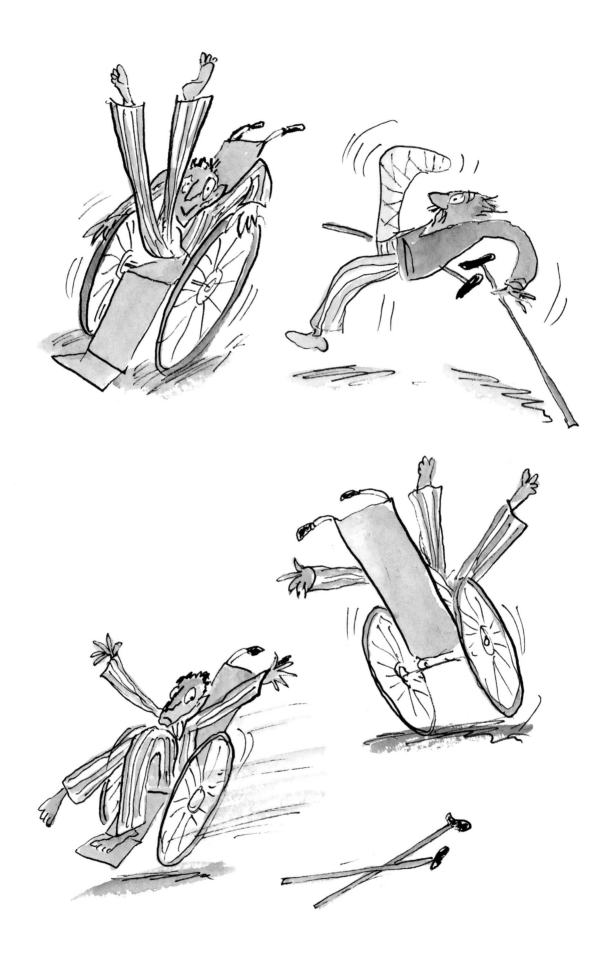

I looked out the window.

It was the first time I had seen the outside world
in two months.
I saw a man go into his house.
I saw cars pass.
I saw a woman come out and water her flowers
on her balcony.

They put me back to bed after that.

The next day,
they said we were going to the gym.
The gym?

First on the walker,
then in the wheelchair,
then off to the gym!

At the gym,
they said they were going to teach me how to stand up by myself.
They said, "Hands behind! Nose over toes!"

And I did it!

The next day, they said they were going to teach me how to walk between parallel bars.

They did.

The next day, they said they were going to teach me how to play soccer between the parallel bars.

They did.

And we played with a balloon,
kicking it to and fro.

I learned how to walk down the hall using the walker.

A few days later,
they said that I had to give up the walker.
I had to use a walking stick.

I was scared.
I thought I would fall over.
I called my walking stick
"Sticky McStickstick."

I loved Sticky McStickstick.
He helped me walk:

move the right leg,
stick down on the right,
move the left leg.

Stick down on the right,
move the left leg,
move the right leg.

Over and over again.

Then they said that
I had to learn how to climb the stairs.

I was gasping and panting all over again.

The stairs were the hardest thing of all.

But now I could walk down the hall
with Sticky McStickstick.

One day a man came and said
that I was using a walking stick too much.
I had to learn how to walk without one.

So I tried.

One step.

Then two steps.

Then three steps.

I was afraid that I would fall over.

But I didn't.

I thought I would try to walk from my bed
to the bathroom without Sticky McStickstick.
Very, very slowly—I did!
I did it!
I was very, very proud that I had done that
all by myself.

I looked back at Sticky McStickstick
by my bed.

I felt that I had deserted him.

Then one day they came to my bedside
and said that I was going home.

I asked if I could take Sticky McStickstick with me.
Yes, that was OK.

When I got home,
there was my lovely family!

Everyone watched to see if I could climb the stairs.

I could!

They watched to see if I could get to the bathroom by myself.

I could!

They watched to see if I could make a cup of tea.

I could!

Sticky McStickstick watched me too.
But sometimes he played hide-and-seek.

It was wonderful being home
with my family.

I practiced walking around the yard.
I practiced walking to the shops.
I did mini squats and stretches.

I can climb the stairs
without holding the banister.

I can make a cup of tea
without leaning on the cupboards.

I can walk to the park to meet up with my son,
his wife, and my granddaughter.

I can do all these things now.

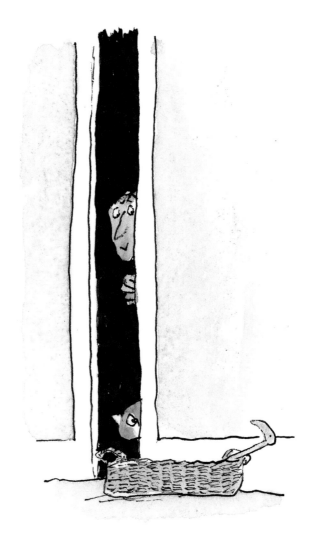

Sticky McStickstick sits in the basket by the front door,
just in case I need him.

I often look at him on my way out,
thinking of the time when he helped me
learn how to walk.

And he reminds me of the kind people
who taught me all those things
right from the time
I couldn't even stand up.

In March 2020, I became very sick with Covid. I became so sick that they had to put me to sleep for forty days. That's a long time doing nothing. It's so long that when I woke up I found that my arms and legs had stopped working. I couldn't stand up. I couldn't walk. Then, bit by bit, the wonderful people in our hospitals taught me how to do these things. When I think about this, I think it's amazing.

My best friend became my walking stick. I learned how to use the stick properly, and it helped me walk again. Until . . . until a day came when I didn't need it anymore.

Maybe you've been sick. Or maybe you know someone who's been sick. When we're sick, we change, don't we? And then we do what we can to get better. People help us. Maybe you are someone who's helped others. Sometimes we get fed up and sad about these things. I find that writing about it helps me. It cheers me up. Sometimes reading about these things helps me too.

I hope this book will give you a chance to think and talk about trying to get better. Maybe you'll write about it too.

MR